*To His Holiness, John Paul II,
a great Pole and a man of God
who is consecrated to Our Lady.*

> *– The Marians of the
>   Immaculate Conception
>   of St. Stanislaus Kostka Province*

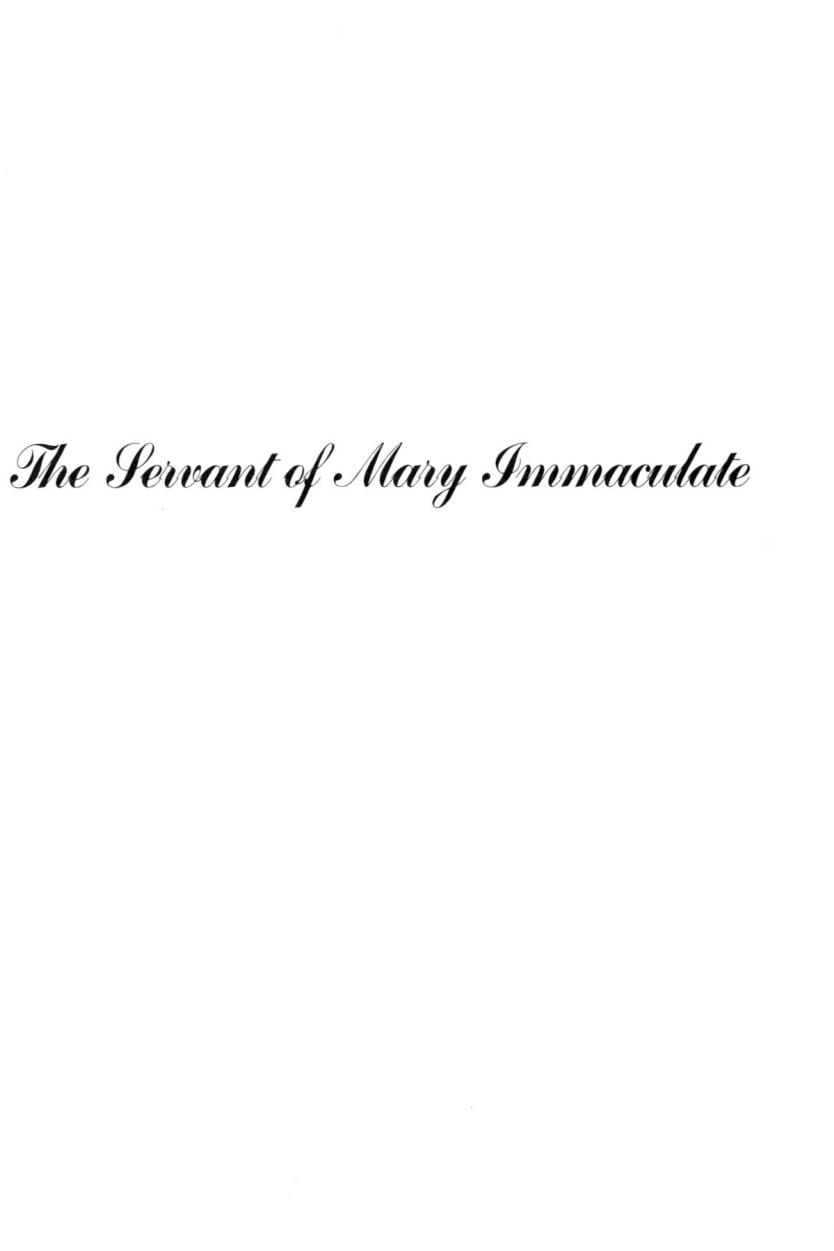

The Servant of Mary Immaculate

The Servant of Mary Immaculate
Father Casimir Wyszyński

Rev. Zygmunt Proczek, MIC

Marians of the Immaculate Conception
Stockbridge, Massachusetts 01263
1997

Imprimi potest for English text
Very Rev. Walter M. Dziordz, MIC, Provincial
Stockbridge, MA, February 2, 1997

Translation and Editing from Polish into English:
Ewa St. Jean

Imprimi potest for original Polish text
Very Rev. Eugeniusz Delikat, MIC
Provincial
Warsaw, November 8, 1985

With the permission of the Metropolitan
Curia in Warsaw, March 7, 1986
No. 915 K 86

Library of Congress Catalog Card Number 96-08195

ISBN 0-944203-27-2

Copyright © 1997 Marians of the Immaculate Conception
All rights reserved.

Project coordinator and art selection:
Br. Andrew R. Mączyński, MIC
Designer for covers and photography insert: *Bill Sosa*
Editing: *Dave Came* and *Tim Flynn*
Typesetting: *BarbaraYork-Condron* and *Pat Menatti*

Front Cover: Portrait of the Venerable Servant of God,
Fr. Casimir Wyszyński, painted by Fr. John Niezabitowski, from
the second half of the 18th century. On display in Goźlin, Poland.

Printed in the United States of America by the Marian Press,
Stockbridge, Massachusetts 01263

TABLE OF CONTENTS

Introduction 7
1. In Search of the Way of Life 11
2. The Steadfast Fulfillment of the Marian Vocation 18
3. Efforts for the Growth of the Marian Family 27
4. Procurator General of the Order in Rome 41
5. Foundation in Portugal 47
6. Defender of the Peasants 56
7. The Propagator of Devotion to Mary 61
8. Awaiting the Beatification 73
9. Prayer for the Beatification 82
10. Prayer for a Special Grace 82
    Information 83

INTRODUCTION

On May 15, 1968, the Primate of Poland, Cardinal Stefan Wyszyński arrived at the parish of Jeziórka near Grójec to venerate the saintly Marian, Father Casimir Wyszyński. In the homily which he delivered on that day, he tried to show that the example of the Servant of God of two centuries earlier speaks to us even today, particularly as it relates to the life of faith, the love of God, the love of Mary Immaculate, and the love of neighbor.

In the Primate's opinion, Father Casimir Wyszyński nurtured his faith through frequent meditations upon the Lord's Passion, and nurtured his love for Mary Immaculate by placing himself at her disposal in the Order of Marians, and by spreading devotion to her in Poland, Lithuania, and Portugal.

He did not limit his activity merely to the work of his own sanctification or to the development of the Order, but he made efforts to bring about the spiritual rebirth of Polish society during the difficult time of Saxon rule. He pointed to Mary in whom he saw the salvation from the deluge of evil which was destroying the Polish nation. Father Casimir came to the conclusion, said Cardinal Wyszyński, that it was necessary to call upon the Blessed Mother in difficult and dangerous times. He believed that only she could help and come to our rescue. He was one of the first to promulgate sweet bondage to the Immaculate Mother of God. He trusted that anything given into her care would never perish.

He knew the needs and complaints of people of all social levels. A man of prayer, he was sensitive to the matters of this earth. Prayer did not block out reality. On the contrary, it made his heart more sensitive to the difficult situation of the oppressed people. By this, he meant farmers first of all. Father Casimir saw people toiling the soil, and, like Christ, drew examples from their lives. He saw the misery of the peasants. He felt the injustices and injuries suffered particularly by the people toiling the land. He understood the importance of the farmers' work and wanted it to be undertaken in love and freedom. Therefore, he fought for the freedom of those who worked toiling the soil.

Father Casimir's zeal and love reached beyond the borders of his homeland. In his desire to strengthen Christ's Kingdom and to spread devotion to Mary Immaculate among other nations, he reached Portugal where, unfortunately, he soon died at the age of 55. A lively memory of his saintly life survives there as is evidenced by the pilgrimages to the tomb of the Servant of God in Balsamao and by the requests for the speedy beatification of the "saintly Pole."

It is our desire that our society, too, should become acquainted with this light which shone in the dark epoch of the Saxon rule. The following biography was prepared with this thought in mind. It includes excerpts from the writings of the Servant of God and materials gathered by the two priests, Joseph Vaiśnora, MIC, and Boleslaus Jakimowicz, MIC, who were put in charge of the beatification causes of candidates to the honors of the altar from the Congregation of Marians. All quotations from Father Casimir's writings have been modernized for the purpose of this book.

Marians of the Immaculate Conception

1. IN SEARCH OF THE WAY OF LIFE

John Casimir and Hedwig (born Zawadzka) Wyszyński belonged to the affluent nobility related to many magnate houses. They were descendants of families characterized by their devotion to religious tradition and piety. It is worth mentioning that John Casimir's own brother Joseph Wyszyński joined the order of the Dominicans. He spent the last years of his life at the church of St. Jacek in Warsaw where he led the Confraternity of the Rosary. On the other hand, Hedwig Wyszyński's three brothers, Ignatius, Wacław, and Dominic Zawadzki, joined the Piarist order.

From 1695, John Casimir and Hedwig Wyszyński were the owners of the estates at Jeziora Wielka and Załęże Wielkie near Grójec. Eight children were born from their marriage, out of which three sons dedicated themselves to the service of God: Andrew John (1684-1754) joined the Piarists, John (1699-1773) joined the Vincentatians, and Januarius Francis, the Marians.

Januarius Francis was born on August 19, 1700 at Jeziora Wielka (presently known as Jeziórka) as the seventh child. During a solemn baptism at the local church at Jeziora Wielka, he was given the names Januarius Francis. His biographers refer to him most often as Francis.

Although well-to-do, his parents could not provide a carefree childhood for their youngest offspring. It was a difficult period in the history of Poland. King Augustus II drew the country into the confusion of the "Northern War" (1701-1709). The Swedish, Saxon, and Russian troops were crossing the Polish territories killing people and looting their possessions. The extent of the devastation was even greater because of the civil war going on between the supporters of Augustus II and Stanislaus Leszcyński, and because of an epidemic ravaging the country at that time which significantly decreased the Polish population.

In 1702, the Swedish army led by King Charles XII invaded the territories of the Polish Republic, introduced their own rule, and plundered the country. When the Swedish troops reached Mazovia, the Wyszyński family had to run away and seek shelter at their relatives' who lived in other regions of the country. The Wyszyńskis' eldest son, Anthony, joined the army fighting against the invaders, and the family feared reprisals. It was only around 1708 that the Wyszyńskis could return to their estate and rebuild the destroyed buildings.

The most important matter was the proper upbringing and education of the children. Therefore, the Wyszyńskis sent their youngest boys, John and Francis, to a school run by the Piarists in Góra Kalwaria. The small distance (about 40 kilometers) between the school and the family home allowed the parents to inquire very frequently as to the boys' progress in their studies. The relations between the Wyszyński family and the Piarists were certainly close and cordial as Mrs. Wyszyński's three brothers were members of this order. One of them, Rev. Wacław Zawadzki was rector of the school in Góra Kalwaria from 1711 to 1714.

Having finished school in Góra Kalwaria, Francis continued his studies at another Piarist school, this time at their college in Warsaw. He distinguished himself with his piety, but experienced a lot of difficulty with his studies. His father, who dreamed of a political career for his son, was not pleased with this.

Since his father treated him badly, Francis decided to go on a pilgrimage to Rome, just like St. Stanislaus Kostka had done a long time before. He set out on this journey without his parents' knowledge. When Francis' mother learned about his escape, she sent her son Michael to look for his brother. Francis had already traveled 70 kilometers. He returned home for the sake of his anxious mother and because of his brother's promise to obtain their father's forgiveness. Indeed, his father showed him a lot of kindness and allowed him to continue his studies in Warsaw.

Upon finishing school, Francis began to work at the chancellery of the town of Warsaw in accordance with his father's wish to prepare himself for a future career. But he was not certain whether this was to be his way of life. For reasons unknown to us today, he made a vow to undertake a pilgrimage to the tomb of St. James of Compostella in Spain. He made this known to his brother Michael, who in turn informed their parents. His father came to Warsaw to talk his son out of the idea of such a pilgrimage. But Francis would not be dissuaded. He did not want to reveal the reason for his vow, either. At that point his father turned to Father Wężyk, a Warsaw official, for help. After a conversation with Francis, Father Wężyk recommended that the young man should make a retreat at the Vincentians. When Francis presented a statement from them that his vow was irrevocable, his father gave permission for the pilgrimage.

Francis put on pilgrim's clothing and was to make his way to Spain via Rome. He was 21 years old at that time. He arrived in Rome in October of 1721, most likely with a group of Polish pilgrims. There are documents indicating that around that time 28 people from Poland, among them Francis and his older brother Joseph, were staying at the Eternal City. On November 1st, they went to confession to Father Sebastian Mulinowicz at St. Peter's Basilica. Perhaps at least a few from the group intended to make a pilgrimage to Compostella.

Francis, however, did not fulfill his original vow. He did reach Spain, but he became so seriously ill that the doctors strongly objected to his continuing the journey. The unfortunate pilgrim had to return to Rome where he obtained permission to change his vow to the visiting of Roman churches and performing acts of mercy. Therefore, he remained in Rome for a while. He performed pious practices and earned his living by copying records in a lawyer's office.

Divine Providence, however, had other plans for him. In the autumn of 1723, Francis by chance met Father Joachim Kozłowski, a Marian, who was in Rome regarding matters of the Congregation, which were to certain degree connected with the Wyszyński family.

For the last few years the Order of Marians had been undergoing a serious ideological crisis which almost ended in the total liquidation of the Marians. According to the intentions of their Founder, the order was to spread devotion to the Immaculate Conception of the Blessed Virgin Mary, bring help to the souls of the departed, and assist parish priests in their work. Contrary to these intentions, Bishop Stanislaus Jacek Święcicki, who conducted the visitation in the Korabiew Forest in 1673, imposed an eremitcal-contemplative character upon the order. The Founder of the Marians, Father Stanislaus Papczyński (1631-1701) did not abandon his original plan, and, in 1699, he obtained from the Holy See the approval of his institute as a congregation dedicated to active apostolic work.

After the death of their Founder, however, the Order of Marians experienced difficulties which almost led to its liquidation. In 1715, Father Matthew Krajewski was elected Superior General of the Order. The members of the electoral chapter expected that this young, energetic, and educated man would contribute to the dynamic growth of the Marians. It happened otherwise. The new Superior General began to denounce his Order before the Papal

Nuncio and before the Bishop of Poznań, even to the point of demanding that the Marian Institute be dissolved.

One of his allies was Francis Wyszyński's older brother Joseph, who had entered the Marian novitiate around 1716, and was given the religious name Alexander. After he left the military troops of King Augustus II, he could not conform with the rigors of the religious life, as he had been accustomed to a less restricted camp life, and the Marian rule even forbade the consumption of alcoholic beverages. Therefore, he gladly supported Father Krajewski's reformist aspirations, and together they denounced the Marians who opposed these new projects before the religious and civil authorities. Moreover, both of them demanded the liquidation of the Order.

The Apostolic Nuncio appointed the Provost of St. John's collegiate church, Bishop Adam Rostkowski, to be Visitator to the Marians. The Bishop closed the novitiate, sent the younger priests of the congregation to assist in pastoral work in various parishes of the diocese of Poznań, to which the region of Mazovia belonged at that time. The reason which Bishop Rostkowski gave to support his decision was the fact that the Constitutions of the Order lacked the official approval of the Holy See. As the result of this visitation, the priests began pastoral work in parishes and some Marian clerics moved to other congregations. Only eight Marians, most of them advanced in age, remained in the monasteries. This difficult period in the history of the Marians, which lasted six years (from 1716 to 1722), is known as "the Rostków Dispersion."

It was the Bishop of Poznań, Peter Tarło who, in his decree of August 1, 1722, ordered all the Marians to return to their monasteries under the threat of excommunication. At the general chapter which took place on August 31, 1722 in Góra Kalwaria, Father Andrew Deszpot was elected Superior General. The new statutes were drawn up and Father Joachim Kozłowski was sent to Rome as Procurator General to obtain the approval of the order by the Pope. It was at the time of his visit to Rome that he met Francis Wyszyński and told him about the damaging activity of his brother Joseph. Upon hearing this account Francis made an almost immediate decision and said to Father Joachim: *I wish to mend what my brother has destroyed. I ask you for a habit.*

On November 18, 1723, in the Church of St. Stanislaus the Bishop and Martyr in Rome, Father Kozłowski received Francis Wyszyński into the Marians. He was given the religious name of Casimir of St. Joseph. In the archives of the Archdiocese of Poznań there is a document of this event which reads among other things: ... *he was vested in a white religious habit by the Very Reverend Father Joachim of St. Anne, at that time assistant and Procurator General of the Order in Rome, and ordered to complete a year of the novitiate at the Korabiew Hermitage in the Polish Kingdom, beginning on the feast of St. Joseph the Confessor at a place appointed by the Most Reverend Father Andrew of St. Matthew, the Superior General.*

For Januarius Francis, now to be known as Casimir of St. Joseph, the period of indecision and searching for the way of life ended with the act of investiture and acceptance to the Marians.

It will be a few years later that he writes to his brother Valerian, a priest in the Order of the Piarists: *I am like a second Saul in this Congregation which had been fought against by our own, that is, by our brother Joseph. The Blessed Mother said to me : "Francis, why are you persecuting me?" Having no more courage to resist these proddings, I had to take the habit in Rome. And now, to be able to propagate this Order of the Most Holy Mother, I, her unworthy servant, must set out on such a long journey.*

2. THE STEADFAST FULFILLMENT OF THE MARIAN VOCATION

Having obtained the approval for the Marian statutes by the Holy See, Father Joachim Kozłowski set out on his journey back to Poland with his companion, Brother Nicholas of St. Martin. They took the candidate to the congregation, Casimir of St. Joseph Wyszyński, with them.

After his return to Poland, Casimir participated in the funeral of his mother, and then, on March 19, 1724, on the Feast of St. Joseph, he entered the novitiate in the

The Steadfast Fulfillment of the Marian Vocation

Korabiew Forest. Seized by the mission of mending the wrongs done to the Order by his brother, he tried to follow the rule and the constitutions as strictly as possible. He was characterized by a spirit of mortification, he did not take meat with his meals, and water was his only beverage.

He noted with sadness that not all the brethren were faithful to the religious life. He even admonished Father Joachim, who was Superior of the monastery at the Korabiew Forest at the time, urging him to be more zealous in watching over the preservation of the statutes, for whose approval he himself had made efforts in Rome, and urged him to preserve himself what he taught to others. It seems that in this way the prophecy of the Founder of the Marians to Father Joachim came true, as he would sometimes say upon observing manifestations of Father Joachim's willfulness: *When you are advanced in years, God will give you a little comb in the Order which will groom you.*

The zealous novice took the opportunity to restore religious discipline and brought about a visitation by the Franciscans who exercised care over the Marians at that time. Michael Wyszyński notes in his biography of his brother that the Marian novices were often sent to perform various chores outside the monastery. This interfered with one's good preparation to the religious life, especially in view of the fact that the priests who stayed in the parishes for a number of years did not always set a good example. Therefore, Casimir, with the mediation of his brother

Michael, asked for the visitation to be conducted. In order to raise the standard of the religious life there, the Visitator, Father James Wolski, of the Order of the Reformati, appointed two Reformati to work at the Korabiew Forest, Father Mansueto Leporini to be the Novice Master, and Father Felician Szadkowski to be the Instructor of Theology.

By demanding strict religious observance, Casimir exposed himself to the displeasure of many of the brethren. It is no wonder, then, that among the opinions about him during his stay in the novitiate some negative voice could always be heard. There were even attempts at prolonging his novitiate, and postponing his religious profession. Even on March 19, 1725, when his family arrived to participate in the ceremony of his profession, yet another vote was hastily organized to decide whether he should be admitted to the vows. Casimir of St. Joseph Wyszyński made his solemn religious profession before Father Joachim Kozłowski, in the presence of Father Michael Gibler and Father Ignatius of St. Matthew, who was the Confessor of the community, and a member of the house council.

Brother Casimir now began intensive preparations for the priesthood. On March 31, 1725, Easter Saturday, in St. John's collegiate church in Warsaw, he received his tonsure and four Minor Orders. On December 22nd of the same year he received the sub-diaconate, and on March 16, 1726, the diaconate. On April 20, 1726, the Bishop of Poznań, John Joachim Tarło, ordained him to the priesthood.

The Steadfast Fulfillment of the Marian Vocation 21

It should be emphasized that as Casimir was preparing himself for the priesthood, he was also engaged in helping other members of the order to pursue their own necessary education by fulfilling his duties as Instructor of Philosophy. Soon after his ordination, he was charged with the duties of Instructor of Theology as well as those of Novice Master, which up to that point had been fulfilled by the Reformati fathers. It was noticed that the young religious priest was endowed with great spiritual and intellectual attributes, and so it was decided that they should be utilized for the good of the Order.

During the General Chapter of June 17, 1728, Father Casimir was made Vice-Superior of the Korabiew Forest monastery and the Novice Master. He fulfilled this duty probably until the end of 1730. However, his great zeal and the offices he held in the community were not to everyone's liking. In particular, those who found themselves outside the monastery during "the Rostków Dispersion" and were then later forced to return, reluctantly accepted the hard style of the religious life.

Through his brother Michael, Father Casimir obtained a summons to Rome where he went as Procurator of the Order along with Father Dionisius Kisieliński and Brother Jacek Wasilewski. He arrived in Rome at the beginning of 1731 and took up his residence at the Franciscan monastery "Ara Coeli." He began efforts to establish a permanent Marian house in the Eternal City. On July 9, 1731, he even signed a contract of perpetual lease of the Madonna Dei Cerchi chapel with Marquis Christopher Cenci, its owner. But the General Council in Poland did not approve this contract because of the high price and the fact that the chapel was located in an unhealthy environment. During his stay in Rome, Father Casimir tended to the matters of his congregation and got acquainted with the lives of other religious orders. He devoted a lot of time to prayer, visiting the churches, reading, and writing.

In 1733 he published a book in Rome titled "Vestigia aeternae felicitatis" (Traces of Eternal Happiness). The book did not survive to our time, so it is not possible to evaluate it today. It appears from the testimonies given by the witnesses in the beatification process that the book was a biography of St. Ignatius of Antioch.

Father Casimir returned to Poland in the first half of 1734. With a new zeal he immersed himself into the current of work for the congregation. He fulfilled the duties of secretary during the chapter of July 3, 1734 at the Korabiew Forest. He was unanimously elected Assistant General; and once again he was given the duty of educating the novices.

At the annual meeting on July 5, 1735, he was made Vice-Superior of the monastery at the Korabiew Forest and Instructor of Moral Theology. On July 10th of the following year, he was entrusted with the responsibility of being Spiritual Director of the Korabiew Forest monastery.

The Steadfast Fulfillment of the Marian Vocation 23

Thus, Father Casimir enjoyed the ever greater confidence of his congregation. Undoubtedly, the number of those who advocated the relaxation of religious observance gradually became smaller and the new generation of Marians, already formed by Father Casimir, was characterized by zeal and enthusiasm. This contributed considerably to the internal and external vigor of the congregation.

During a session of the General Chapter in Skórzec on December 12, 1737, Father Casimir Wyszyński was unanimously elected Superior General of the Order. The young and dynamic General of the Marians fulfilled this honorable duty for three years and was instrumental in the growth of his religious family. When all the offices were distributed at the chapter in Skórzec, Father Casimir detained the delegates for deliberations and for a discussion of a program of work which he had drawn up in 29 points. The council approved it in its entirety. He declared that he did not intend to exercise his authority like a dictator but in consultation with the council. He remarked that he accepted the responsibility of the faithful preservation of the statutes and the rule. He promised to make certain that the decisions of the chapter would not remain a dead letter, but would be implemented.

As the Superior General of the Order, he demanded that the superiors of the monasteries set an example of the religious life for others, that they make certain that religious exercises be performed conscientiously, and that they watch over the younger brethren. He also ordered that the superiors take care of their subordinates and supply them with necessary provisions, thereby protecting them from any transgression against the vow of poverty. Furthermore, he encouraged the superiors to deal with their subordinates in a fatherly manner without showing impatience, and without being guided by ambition.

Every three months the economes of the various monasteries were to make financial reports to their superiors and the latter were to present such reports to the Superior General and his council at an annual meeting. It was also to be the responsibility of the superiors to attend to the maintenance and repair of the monasteries. In his concern for the preservation of discipline in the monasteries, he emphasized that it was necessary for the Marian students to make proper use of their time. Lecturers were obliged to use the hours dedicated to lectures conscientiously and to watch over the students' recreation time. Father Casimir ordered that those neglecting their studies should be punished, even in public. Professors were to set a good example for the students.

As the Superior General of the Marians, he placed special emphasis on formation in the novitiate. He decided that no one other than the Superior General had the right to control the novice master. He drew up appropriate regulations for the novices and separated their quarters from those of the professed members. He ordered that nobody should leave the monastery without the definite permission of the superior or his substitute, and that those sent on a longer journey should be supplied with letters of recommendation.

In December of 1737, Father Casimir Wyszyński addressed a letter to all of his subordinates. He wrote in it that God chose him in spite of his unworthiness and placed on him the duty of shepherding. He accepted this office to serve the Lord and to prepare the flock left in his care for the coming of the Lord. Following the example of St. John the Baptist, he called upon the Marians to make the pathways straight and to prepare new roads.

Father Casimir realized that the religious life makes sense only when those in religious vows steadfastly follow the road of the evangelical counsels as presented by the statutes of the order. Therefore, his first and most important concern was to lay strong foundations for the spiritual life and to encourage perfection in the religious life. He realized that he would not have much of an effect upon the older Marians who had given in to the improper influences of the times during the "Rostków Dispersion". He put all his hopes in the formation of the younger Marians and watched over the proper upbringing of the novices with an even greater zeal.

He strongly recommended that all the Marians imitate the Blessed Virgin Mary and Father Stanislaus Papczyński, the Founder of the Marians. While he lived in Rome from 1731 to 1733, he translated a treaty titled "De imitatione Mariae Virginis" (On the Imitation of the Virgin Mary) written by a Spanish Jesuit, Francis Arias. In 1749, he made the translation of this work available to the Polish reader. One might surmise that this book served Father Wyszyński as a commentary to the "Rule of the Ten Virtues of the Blessed Virgin Mary," by which the Marians were bound at that time. Upon announcing the general visitation, Father Wyszyński wrote in 1749 that he wanted to see whether the Marians did indeed live in the Marian spirit and whether they imitated the virtues of their Patroness.

Like no one else before him, Father Casimir took care to spread the honor of Father Stanislaus Papczyński, the Founder of the Marians. To a great degree, Father Joachim Kozłowski was responsible for the fact that the Founder's beatification process had not been started. Therefore, Father Casimir himself made efforts to bring about the elevation to the honors of the altar of the first Polish founder of a religious order.

During the chapter of August 8, 1741, Father Casimir was entrusted with the office of the Superior of the monastery in Góra Kalwaria. With the financial help in the amount of one thousand Polish zlotys which he had received from his brother Michael, he built a new monastery and renovated the Church of the Cenacle in Góra Kalwaria. It was in this church that the earthly remains of Father Stanislaus Papczyński had been buried in soggy ground. After obtaining the permission of the church authorities, Father Casimir moved them to a new tomb.

Father Casimir wanted in a very special way to familiarize Polish society with the person of the Founder of the Marians. He persuaded Father Lucas Rosolecki, the dean of the Piarists in Vilnius to write Father Papczyński's biography. During one of the Marian chapters, Father Casimir suggested that an engraving with Father Papczyński's image should be made and spread among the people. While he was staying in Rome in 1751, he gathered information regarding the procedure of the beatification process. He urged the superiors of the time not to neglect their efforts to bring about the elevation to the honors of the altar of their Founder.

He directly associated these efforts to the spiritual and physical growth of his religious family and the cultivation of devotion to Mary. He wrote to his beloved disciple, Father Casimir Polak: *Our demise is certain if should we doubt the sanctity of our Founder and neglect to spread the honor which is due to him; for in so doing we cast discredit on such a great Servant of God and on devotion to the Blessed Mother.*

His awareness of these matters became a source of wise and far-reaching decisions which Father Casimir would make after he had been elected Superior General of the Marians for a second time.

3. EFFORTS FOR THE GROWTH OF THE MARIAN FAMILY

Father Casimir Wyszyński was the Superior of the

monastery in Góra Kalwaria for six years and, at the same time, as a former Superior General, actively participated in the administration of the Order. Therefore, it surprised no one when on June 19, 1747, at the General Chapter in Skórzec, he was elected Superior General yet again. He continued to take care of the proper formation of the Marians, of acquiring new candidates and establishing new religious houses.

He had already made efforts to attract new vocations to the Marians during his stay in Rome from 1731 to 1733. A few Italian and Spanish candidates did apply, but they soon withdrew due to the fact that it was impossible to establish a monastery in the Eternal City at the time. It was only during Father Casimir's second stay in Rome in 1751 that he recruited Raphael de Buffa of Piedmont who became a dedicated worker of the Order in Portugal.

During his first term as Superior General, he often sent Father Casimir Polak, who was of Czech descent, to Prague with the mission of recruiting new candidates. Thanks to this persistent work, six candidates joined the Marians in 1738, five in 1739, and another eleven Czechs in 1740. The Czech vocations became a valuable intellectual and spiritual contribution to the Congregation of Marians. Such persons as Casimir Polak, Isidor Taudt, Alexy Fischer, John Kanty Szkrafer, Benedict Hönig, John Nepomucen Czermak, and the three Machaczeks brought honor both to the congregation and to the Czech nation by their lives and works. Following Father

Efforts for the Growth of the Marian Family 29

Casimir as their ideal, they worked very fruitfully in Poland and Portugal. They paved the way for others.

More Czechs would come to the Marians until the end of the 18th century. Three of them in particular rendered great services to the order. Father Candid Spourny, one of the most courageous Procurator Generals of the Marians, who was very enterprising and characterized by an exceptional ease at winning friends and benefactors, managed to procure for the Marians the Church of St. Vitus in Rome together with the adjacent Cistercian monastery. It was there that the permanent office of the Procurator General was established. It existed there until 1798 when all foreigners were expelled from Italy by the Napoleonic troops. Father Joseph Mraas, a splendid organizer, who was always warmly received and especially welcomed in the homes of magnates, was a Superior General of the congregation for four years. Father Clement Reddig, who served as Novice Master for many years, educated young generations of Marians in the spirit of Father Wyszyński.

Father Casimir hoped to attract candidates of other nationalities as well. In his plans to develop the congregation, he reached out to Lithuania and Ruthenia, from where, in time, new vocations would arrive. The Congregation of Marians owes to Father Casimir Wyszyński its more universal character. The Czechs, Italians, Lithuanians, Ruthenians, Hungarians, and French who applied to join the Marians would spend their novitiate in Poland, to get acquainted with Polish culture, language, and traditions. During the years 1786 to 1790, after the Marians had been released from supervision by the Reformati, separate novitiates were officially established for Poland and Lithuania. Later, Father Casimir personally went to Portugal and established a Marian monastery there. He also had plans to establish the Marians in Brazil; but this would only be realized during the second half of the 20th century.

Attracting these new and valuable vocations to the congregation turned the attention of the Polish society to the Marians and to the person of Father Wyszyński. In the beatification process of the Servant of God, Father Taudt stated: *The congregation grew to such a degree that the Polish magnates admired such a numerous host of the religious and congratulated Father Wyszyński, for it was due to his work and efforts that the Marians, until now little known, grew to such a great number in Poland.*

Great love for the congregation and its Founder was the basis of Father Casimir's zeal to attract vocations. He was able to instill his love and zeal for the development of the Order into the hearts of young generations who would continue his work. During the years 1751 to 1781, the number of Marians would triple.

Father Wyszyński took care to obtain new foundations for the Marians. In spite of the fact that many Czechs were joining the congregation, nowhere is it written that attempts were made to establish a Marian monastery in

Czech territory. But Father Casimir was instrumental in establishing the Marian monastery in Raśna near Brześ:, on the territory of the Grand Duchy of Lithuania. His efforts in this matter, begun in 1735, came to a successful conclusion only in 1749.

George Matuszewicz, the Subprefect of Stoklin and the heir to the estate of Raśna, having met Father Wyszyński, decided to found a monastery for the Marians on his property. His son Martin wrote in his memoirs: *My father, God rest his soul, always had a great devotion to the Blessed Virgin, such that when Father Casimir Wyszyński, a very pious priest from the Order of Marians, visited him in Bębnów in 1735 in response to his inquiries about their rule, my father decided to found a monastery for them in Raśna.*

Martin supported his father's plans, but his mother, Theresa, born "Kępska," the daughter of the chamberlain of Płock, opposed such an idea. She constantly reproached her husband suggesting that he was a spendthrift and squandered money on pious causes. She reproached Martin, too, for supporting and even encouraging his father in this matter. When the foundation was finally established, Theresa Matuszewicz left for Goślice in the Płock district and never returned to Raśna again.

This Marian foundation encountered more serious difficulties from the local church authorities. The Bishop of Łuck, Francis Anthony Kobielski made a formal protest against the Marian foundation in Raśna, imposed a 1000-

zloty fine upon Matuszewicz, and excommunicated him for starting to build the church and the monastery without the permission of the church authorities. In his writings, Father Wyszyński himself mentioned the Bishop's hostile attitude. He recalled that the Bishop was rather favorable to Father Stephen Turczynowicz at the time, who was illegally attempting to found an order of baptized Jews based on the Marian rule. Bishop Kobielski even tried to persuade Matuszewicz to transfer his foundation in Raśna to them. When his efforts did not succeed, he imposed ecclesiastical sanctions upon him. The Bishop, in turn, was later suspended from exercising his authority by the Holy See, and it was only after the personal intercession of King Augustus III that the Bishop's authority to run the diocese was restored.

Martin Matuszewicz interceded at the Apostolic Nunciature in Warsaw asking that the excommunication imposed upon his father by the Bishop be revoked and that permission be granted to continue work on the foundation. He obtained support in the matter from Prince Michael Czartoryski who considered himself Father Wyszyński's friend. The fine and the excommunication were revoked and Matuszewicz was told to turn to the local church authorities to obtain permission for the foundation.

It was only in 1747 that Bishop Kobielski signed a so-called "instrument," which allowed the Marians to settle in Raśna. He appointed Father Glinka, the Archdeacon of Brześć, to install them there officially. But it became necessary to wait for another two years. It was only at the request of Father Wyszyński that Bishop Kobielski arrived on June 8, 1749 to consecrate the church and solemnly install the Marians on their new foundation.

Father Casimir personally participated in this celebration, and in his letter to all the Marians dated June 3, 1749, he shared the following message: *I also ask your fervent prayers for the installation of our fathers at Raśna which will take place on a Sunday in the Octave of Corpus Christi. As I was returning from Vilnius, I unexpectedly received the decision of the most noble Bishop of Łuck, stating that due to other engagements this matter should not be postponed any longer.*

During the first session of the annual meeting at the Korabiew Forest on June 28th of the same year, Father Wyszyński informed the General Council that Bishop Kobielski had approved the foundation in Raśna and given permission to establish a Marian monastery there. When he asked the members of the council whether they would give their consent to do so, they answered unanimously that not only did they give their consent, but they heartily thanked the Superior General for all his efforts thus far. It was ordered that the report from the celebration and the ceremony of the installation of the Marians in Raśna be read in the refectory in the presence of the entire community.

But, in 1750, the first superior of the Marians in Raśna, Father Isidor Taudt, a very tactful, well-educated, and pious man, still had to overcome quite a lot of difficulties with their benefactor himself. Matuszewicz felt that the Marians were not fulfilling the conditions accepted by Father Wyszyński. Eight Marians were supposed to reside at the monastery. In accordance with this agreement, the general council sent four priests and four clerics. Matuszewicz did not want to accept clerics who were completing their studies, but demanded eight priests. Moreover, he was offended that Princess Czartoryski had been given a Marian for her chaplain while he had been refused such an honor. In time, these matters were cleared up and, following their benefactor's death in 1754, relations with the Matuszewicz family settled down. For many years to come, the monastery in Raśna served as a house of studies for clerics and was one of the richer, thriving houses until it was liquidated in 1864.

The second foundation obtained by Father Wyszyński was also located in the Duchy of Lithuania, in Staropol, whose name was changed in time to Mariampol, after the Marians. Due to his friendship with Theodore Czartoryski, the Bishop of Poznań, Father Casimir became acquainted with his brother Michael, later a chancellor of the Grand Duchy of Lithuania. As Prince Michael got to know Father Wyszyński better, he very much appreciated his intellectual abilities, and formed a very positive opinion about the Marians. He asked them to send an appropriate candidate for the office of his court chaplain and theologian. Father Benedict Hönig, of Czech descent, was selected. He was not only an outstanding theologian, but was

Efforts for the Growth of the Marian Family

also a man of great intellectual aptitude who spoke several European languages, and was endowed with an affable nature. The Marians served as court chaplains for the Czartoryski family from 1749 up to 1853. The last chaplain, Father John Dziewulski, faithfully accompanied Prince Adam Czartoryski when he emigrated, traveling with him to various European capitals.

Michael Czartoryski often visited and went hunting with the Butler counts at Preny in Lithuania. Father Hönig, accompanying the Prince, made acquaintance with Frances (born Szczuk) Butler who intended to build a church on her estate and settle a religious community there. Their task would be to exercise pastoral care over the local people as the estate was situated rather far away from the church in Preny.

At Father Hönig's suggestion, the countess wrote a letter to Father Wyszyński, then Superior General, offering the Marians a foundation in Staropol. The Superior General wanted to investigate personally the possibility of establishing a Marian house there. He had already made plans to travel to Lithuania because of the aforementioned Father Stephen Turczynowicz, who was organizing a religious association known by the name "Mariae vitae," making illegal use of the Marian rule and statutes. Father Wyszyński took this opportunity to meet with the Butlers and, after inspecting the estate, promised to send one priest immediately and six more after the monastery was built.

During the annual council at the Korabiew Forest, Father Wyszyński asked the general council to consider a proposal to accept this new foundation. The council gave its consent taking into consideration not only the possibility of establishing a new religious house, but also the greater opportunity to spread devotion to the Immaculate Conception of the Blessed Virgin Mary.

According to the contract, Father Wojciech Strach, a Czech, arrived at Staropol with one lay brother in April of 1750. On September 26, 1752, another priest, Father Jacek Wasilewski, was sent to assist them, and, in 1755, Father Francis Raabe, a Czech, and a lay brother, Thomas Dering. At first they lived in a house by the wooden church. Countess Butler ordered that household quarters be built, and bequeathed to the Marians about 11 acres of land as well as the grounds between the rivers Sheshupa and Jeś, upon which the Marians would later begin to build the town of Mariampol. The construction of a monastery which could house a greater number of people was finished only in 1758. The solemn installation of the Marians in Mariampol by the Dean of Olita, Father Wnorowski, with the participation of Countess Butler and her son Michael, in the presence of the pastors of the local parishes, took place on September 13, 1758.

The monastery in Mariampol played an important role in the history of the Marians. A novitiate was established there in which new initiates of the religious would prepare themselves to the service of God and Mary Immaculate.

Efforts for the Growth of the Marian Family

The Marians received official permission to open the novitiate from Father Clement Panormitano, the Apostolic Commissary of the Franciscans, who, by the authority of the Holy See, drew up the erection document. This was the crown jewel of Father Wyszyński's efforts, who attended to this matter during his stay in Rome in 1752. There are reasons to believe that the novitiate in Mariampol was open as early as December 5, 1754 and that it was occupied mostly by Lithuanians. Father Wyszyński remembered this foundation and its benefactress. From Rome he sent relics of the Holy Cross for the church there under the same name, and, for Countess Butler, relics of her patroness, St. Frances of Rome.

It is worth mentioning that the Mariampol monastery was the only one which the tsarist authorities allowed the Marians to keep after the Cassation Order of 1864. The General Superiors as well as all other members resided there. By 1909, only the Superior General himself remained alive, and it was by his approval that the renovation of the Marians by Father George Matulewicz took place in hiding from the authorities.

The third foundation which the Marians owe to Father Wyszyński's efforts was a monastery in Berezdów, in Volhynia. Under circumstances less familiar to us, Father Casimir met Prince John Kajetan Jabłonowski, the governor of the district of Braclaw. The prince decided to found a church and monastery for the Marians on his estate. The choice was Berezdów, a little town on the river Korczyk, a few kilometers away from the town Korzec.

During the preparatory processes for the beatification of Father Casimir Wyszyński, conducted in Poland, Fathers Taudt, Czermak, Wasilewski, and Bujalski unanimously testified that Father Wyszyński made efforts to obtain this foundation *in order to spread devotion to God and to the honor of the Immaculate Conception ever more, he found pious benefactors, who, upon seeing in his person a fullness of virtues and attributes founded the monasteries in Raśna, Mariampol, and Berezdów*. This opinion is confirmed in a letter written by John Kajetan Jabłonowski, dated April 14, 1755, to the Superior General of the Marians, Father Kajetan Wetycki. He undertakes an agreement to build a monastery in which seven religious would live.

The monastery in Berezdów must have been ready by the first half of 1755 because it was during the annual meeting of the Marians in Goźlin on June 28th of that year that Father Benon Bujalski and Father Joachim Stanisławski were appointed to move in there. A year later, at the annual meeting in Raśna on June 26, 1756, a letter from Prince Jabłonowski regarding the Berezdów foundation was read, and Father Długołęcki and Brother Onuphrius Kierski were sent to live in the new monastery. The solemn installation on the foundation in Berezdów took place on May 20, 1760, upon the completion of the construction of the monastery and the Church of the Immaculate Conception of the Blessed Virgin Mary.

The Marians worked in Berezdów until 1832 when many of the so-called nieetatowe' monasteries were abolished by a tsarist ukase. The Marians had done pastoral work there and assisted the local clergy. They had quite a number of vocations from Volhynia. During the years 1787 to 1790, they even tried to establish a novitiate there, and wrote to Rome in this regard. It is not known why this project was abandoned. It seems that the partitioning of Poland became an obstacle. In the Berezdów monastery, there had also lived Ruthenians of the Eastern rite, most of whom adopted the Latin rite. For a certain period of time the Marians had one more monastery in Volhynia which they called a residence, in Ostrzyków or Samczyki. Both these places were located on two sides of the river Słucz, but comprised a whole.

In the 18th century this locality belonged to the Chojecki family. It was most likely from this family that one Marian, Father Peter Chojecki, came from. He died on November 28, 1759 in Goźlin. According to the testimony of Father Benon Bujalski, this second foundation was also due to Father Wyszyński's efforts, even though it was realized somewhat later: *During the lifetime of the Servant of God Casimir and during his charge of our monasteries in Poland, a new foundation, that of the monastery in Ostrzyków in Ruthenia, was added; but this foundation was realized only in the later years.*

On the basis of a document drawn up on January 5, 1752, Prince Sanguszko approved the borders of the farm, the garden, and the grounds on which the monastery and the church were to be built. However, the foundation contract was signed between Francis Casimir Chojecki and the Superior General of the Marians, Father Jacek Wasilewski, only on March 4, 1767, in Policzyńce. Chojecki's son, Joseph, joined the Marians in Ostrzyków and was given the religious name of Vincent. Yet he remained a so-called perpetual cleric because following his profession, it turned out that he suffered from epilepsy. He bore his illness patiently during his ten year stay in the Order. He died on May 25, 1780, in his native Ostrzyków. It was probably for his sake that the Chojecki family conceived of a foundation in the estate which they administered.

The foundation in Ostrzyków did not survive long because the Chojecki's lost Samczyki in 1782 to Stanislaus Lubomirski. Although in the official documents the monastery is referred to as a residence in Ostrzyków, it happened to be located in Samczyki. After he had taken possession of Samczyki, Lubomirski did not want to recognize the foundation and all that had been bequeathed to the monastery. The Marians had to leave Samczyki in 1789. Two years later the walls of the church and the monastery were torn down and all traces of the Marians in Samczyki disappeared.

On November 12, 1750, Father Wyszyński turned over the care of the Marians to the new Superior General, Father Kajetan Wetycki. The Servant of God, Father Casimir must have felt extremely grateful to God for allowing him to contribute to the renewal and spiritual vigor of the Marians. Having divested himself of the duties of the Superior General, Father Casimir went to Rome and Portugal and undertook new efforts to establish the Marians in the world. This was the last, extremely fruitful stage of his life.

4. PROCURATOR GENERAL OF THE ORDER IN ROME

At the general chapter on November 12, 1750, Father Casimir Wyszyński was made Procurator General of the Order in Rome. His most important task there was to defend the Order against the illegal activities of Father Stephen Turczynowicz, who founded a congregation under the name of "Mariae vitae." Its members were baptized Jews, both men and women, whom Turczynowicz dressed in the white Marian habit. Their activities confused the Polish society which began to look at the Marians with suspicion. When leaving for Rome to take care of this matter, Father Wyszyński also intended to begin efforts for the beatification of the Founder of the Marians and to establish a Marian monastery in the Eternal City.

He arrived there in the company of Father John Kanty Szkraffer. Father Wyszyński's stay in Rome between the years 1751 to 1753 was extremely busy. In the Congregation for the Propagation of the Faith, he managed to bring the conflict with Father Turczynowicz to a happy end. The Congregation issued a ban forbidding the members of the congregation "Mariae vitae" to wear the Marian habit.

Father Wyszyński also obtained the instructions he sought as to how to begin the beatification process of Father Stanislaus Papczyński and sent them to Poland. He insisted that neither time nor money should be spared to conduct this process and believed that the future of the congregation depended on this effort. He attributed the success and development of the Order to the intercession of the Founder whom he himself loved with the love of a son. He insisted in his letters to the Superior General that this matter should be promptly attended to while the handful of eyewitnesses of Father Papczyński's life and work was still alive. He claimed that the matter of the beatification was directly connected to the spreading of devotion to the Immaculate Conception and to the growth of the congregation.

He also pointed out that, in the event an appropriate person could not be found to assume the tasks in this cause for beatification, he would readily do so and forgo his journey to Portugal. He stressed, however, that *for the love of God he was not alone in the congregation. Why should not what is most beneficial to us take place without me?* He emphasized that no one should be afraid of the costs involved for this particular purpose. To the contrary, Divine Providence would be manifest, assisting them through the support of benefactors, as long as the work was undertaken. He also believed that the Marians would find considerable help in Portugal.

Father Casimir asked the Superior General to familiarize the members of the council with the contents of his letter, and he himself wrote to two of them, Father Ladislaus and Father Casimir, insisting that devotion to Father Papczyński be propagated. He complained that he was painfully wounded by such sarcastic remarks about the Marians as: *This congregation originated in Poland and in Poland it will end.*

In his farewell letter to the Bishop of Poznań, he asked the bishop to support the beatification cause of the Founder of the Marians, who in his diocese *for many years worked for God's glory and for the salvation of the souls, and who fell asleep in the Lord and was buried in Góra (Kalwaria).* Father Wyszyński tried to convince the bishop that starting this process would contribute to the growth of the order and bring honor to the Homeland and to the diocese of Poznań.

In his letter to Father Ambrose, who was staying in Góra, he encouraged him *not to spare any effort for the great Servant of God and the particular venerator of the Blessed Mother.* He encouraged Father Norbert, the Superior in Góra Kalwaria, *to make every effort to spread Father Papczyński's honor, especially as the Superior of the place where such a precious Treasure lies.*

Father Wyszyński also took care to commission an appropriate portrait of Father Papczyński. He had a lot of trouble with this because the artist did not render the likeness of the Founder very well. Moreover, he fell ill and it became necessary to find another artist who made some alterations.

During his stay in Rome, Father Casimir obtained from the Holy See many privileges for the Order of Marians and for its friends. He also went about in search of a church attached to a monastery, so that the Marians could settle in the Eternal City. He took pains to recruit candidates of Italian descent. His "Personal Records of the Activities of the Servant of God, Casimir Wyszyński, in Rome and his Notes Concerning the Canonization of the Founder" as well as the fragments of his "Diary" that remain to this day, give one an idea of his undertakings at that time.

Before he left for Rome, Father Wyszyński had obtained letters of recommendation from King Augustus III and Prince Czartoryski to Cardinal Colonna, the protector of the Franciscans, with whom the Marians were affiliated at the time, asking that he look into the possibility of obtaining a foundation for the Marians. Father Wyszyński's initial attempts to meet Cardinal Colonna and Pope Benedict XIV in person brought no result. Hence, having obtained letters of recommendation from the Polish minister Lagnasco, Father Wyszyński set out for Naples accompanied by Father John Kanty Szkraffer to ask the Queen of Naples, the daughter of King Augustus III, to intercede for him with the Pope. This trip proved to be of no avail. The queen refused to intercede on behalf of the Marians.

After some time, however, Father Wyszyński managed to make contact with the Pope and Cardinal Colonna. He submitted a letter to the Holy Father asking him for a place to settle in Rome. At the same time, Father Casimir asked Cardinal Colonna for his support in purchasing the Church of St. Bibiana. The church belonged to the Chapter of the Blessed Mother Major Basilica, and the cardinal was a member of this chapter. He found an attorney, Peter Pruski, who agreed to negotiate with the chapter on his behalf. He also asked for the help of Father Pepe, a Jesuit, who was very influential in the Vatican. All of these efforts turned out to be futile. At the beginning of November, 1751, Father Wyszyński was informed that the Chapter of the Blessed Mother Major would not sell the Church of St. Bibiana.

The Procurator General of the Marians did not give up, however. He turned his attention to the Church of Santa Maria in Dominica or Navicella located just outside the city. This church was very much to his liking. In his "Record of the Activities" he presented his arguments as to why the Marians should try to obtain this place. It is a church dedicated to the Blessed Mother. There is a mosaic there, that can be found nowhere else in the world, depicting the apostles dressed all in white, the color of the Marian habit. He learned from Brother Gianbattista, a Franciscan whom he had befriended, that the church belonged to the Basilian monks, who were having difficulties maintaining it because their Eastern Rite was foreign to the local people. With the permission of the Sacred Congregation for the Propagation of the Faith, the Basilians were presently collecting contributions from the Christian countries in order to purchase a different place. In the meantime, the church was almost completely abandoned and it was only occasionally that some priests would celebrate the Mass there.

For these reasons, Father Wyszyński engaged Peter Pruski, the attorney, to obtain this church for the Marians. But all of this information proved to be erroneous. Not only hadn't the Basilians abandoned this place, they did not intend to sell the church, either. The Franciscan brother mentioned earlier took Father Wyszyński to another church, one belonging to the Brotherhood of Saddlers, but again, they were unsuccessful.

It was, therefore, a great joy for the Procurator General of the Marians finally to be received by the Holy Father, Benedict XIV, at an audience on November 29, 1751. During this audience he presented the present situation of the order to the Holy Father, he discussed the matter of Father Turczynowicz, he asked to obtain special indulgences and relics, and submitted three memorials, one of which regarded the settling of the Marians in the Eternal City: *(the Holy Father) discussed the matter with me and when I told him that we did not have a place to live here in Rome, he said: "Look for the place and we will help you." When I mentioned to him the church of Santa Maria in Navicella, he said: "You are doing the right thing, I approve and give my blessing" and he patted me and made the sign of the Cross on my head. O, how I rejoiced and felt revived after this audience ...*

Since the purchase of the Church of Santa Maria in Navicella proved impossible, Father Wyszyński was forced to look for another place. He even found a church and a house with a vineyard at Prince Barberini's, but he could not afford to make an immediate payment in the amount of 110 *zechini*, which was about 2,000 Polish zlotys. In March of 1752, negotiations regarding the purchase of the Church of St. Sebastian were successfully under way but were later suspended to attend to the matter of Father Turczynowicz.

Despite his many attempts and efforts, Father Wyszyński was never able to obtain a permanent residence for the Marians during his two-year stay in Rome. This would be accomplished only in 1779 by Father Kandyd Spourny, who purchased the Church of St. Vitus and the adjacent Cistercian monastery.

5. FOUNDATION IN PORTUGAL

In March of 1752, Father Wyszyński received the news that the King of Portugal had invited the Marians to his kingdom. He wrote a joyful letter to the Superior General about this matter: *Glory be to God, Our Lord, that for the honor of the Immaculate Conception of the Blessed Virgin, He does not forget us, who bear this same title; rather, in all adversities, He consoles these humble ones, and those scorned by all; and He raises up the poor from their misery to place them among princes. The King of Portugal writes to the Procurator General in Spain demanding that he should bring our friars from Poland to Portugal as he wants to honor us with a royal foundation.*

Father Wyszyński insisted that someone should be sent from Poland as soon as possible. He suggested that he himself, Father John Kanty Szkraffer, a Czech, and *another Pole with him for the honor of the Polish nation* should be sent. He wrote in detail what they should take with them to Portugal and suggested that they *seek the recommendation and support of the Polish lords, so that they would assist us in this matter and fund our journey to Portugal for our Homeland's greater honor and respect. For it is a great honor for the Polish Kingdom that a Polish order of religious should be summoned by such a monarch.*

Father Wyszyński sent letters about the matter to an official in Warsaw, Father Anthony Casimir Ostrowski (later, the Primate of Poland); to the Bishop of Poznań, Theodore Czartoryski; to the Castellan of Rawa, Felician Trzciński, his close friend; to his alumnus, Father Casimir Polak; and to his own brother, Michael. He also wrote several times to the Superior General, Father Kajetan Wetycki.

While still in Rome, he kept insisting that a final decision be made. He did not want to squander this opportunity to spread the honor of Mary Immaculate. Concerned

Foundation in Portugal

about the lack of news from Poland, Father Wyszyński wrote about his worries to the Superior General of the order on July 15, 1752. Everyone was asking whether the Marians had already arrived from Poland, and he could not even say whether they had left at all. For this reason he was considered to be an irresponsible man, acting on his own. Therefore, he remarked in his letter: *I wish that such matters which are to serve God's greater glory and the promotion of the Order would not be postponed until later, until a council or a chapter. The Superior General may decide these matters of his own authority.*

Father Wyszyński finally received the news that Father John Szkraffer was appointed to go to Portugal. Father Wyszyński insisted that he should get there as soon as possible, even if he had to take a loan for the journey. He claimed that they could not delay taking over the foundation in Portugal and spreading devotion to Mary Immaculate. When he found out that Father Szkraffer tried to excuse himself on account of his poor health, he reproachfully confided in the Superior General that he did not know who would work when the young excuse themselves due to poor health or unwillingness.

On August 6, 1752, he received the news from the General that his own candidacy for Portugal had been accepted and that Father Benon Bujalski was appointed to be his companion. Father Alexy Fischer was to assume the duties of the Procurator General in Rome. Both arrived in Rome on November 2nd and took their residence together with Father Wyszyński at the "Ara Coeli" monastery. It was only in May of 1753 that Father Casimir and Father Benon set out for the new foundation. They arrived in Spain by ship, then by land, and reached Lisbon in Portugal that October.

The first pieces of information about Polish Marians in Portugal date back to October 2, 1753. Anthony da Silva e Sousa, Procurator General of the state archives and the guardian of the royal children wrote: *On October 2, 1753, as I was traveling from the city of Beja to Mertoli, a place located on the outskirts of the kingdom, I met the Servant of God, Father Casimir and his companion on a hill, sitting in the shadow of a green oak tree, sheltered from the heat of the sun. I approached them and greeted them. I did not know their language, and they did not speak a word of Portuguese, either. Nevertheless I understood the Servant of God perfectly. He said that he was coming from Poland and going to Lisbon, having been called there to establish his religious order; that he was carrying letters to the king; and that he was traveling on foot all the time.* This is a testimony gathered during the information process conducted in Portugal regarding the sanctity of Father Casimir. It should be mentioned that Anthony da Silva e Sousa remained a great friend and benefactor of the Marians in Portugal until his death.

When the two travelers reached Lisbon on October 10, 1753, they began to look for the man who invited the Marians to Portugal on behalf of the king, promising

Foundation in Portugal 51

them the best possible conditions. They soon found out that they had been deceived. They learned that nobody at the royal court or any person of note in Portugal had ever thought of a foundation for the Marians.

The whole affair proved to be a ruse of Father Anthony de Souza Salazar who had himself tried to found an order of the Immaculate Conception. His efforts to do so had brought no results thus far. When he learned from the Franciscans about the existence of the Marians of the Immaculate Conception, he decided to bring them to Portugal to realize his own plans. The Marians from Poland were only to be a tool in Salazar's hand. He treated them very badly, insulted and humiliated them, and thereby experienced their humility and sanctity. Father Benon Bujalski became seriously ill and decided that it was imperative that he should return to Poland. When his health allowed, he set out on his journey on December 26, 1753, to return home by land. Father Wyszyński decided to remain in Portugal.

In his letter of June 13, 1754, he wrote to the Superior General of the Marians in Poland: *As Father Benon left for Poland on December 26, 1753, please let me know whether he has arrived. Following Father Benon's departure, I had to break with Father Salazar because I could not arrange anything with him regarding the promotion of our Order. The Lord God, however, gave me protectors who, from Father Salazar's hand, almost by force, opened for me a way to better promote our Order.*

Father Wyszyński freed himself from Father Salazar with the help of two persons, Salvador Marcel de Figueiredo y Sylva, a landowner and the king's courtier, and John of God of the Immaculate Conception (Joao de Deus da Conceicao), who had also made attempts to found an order in honor of the Immaculate Conception. The two of them obtained from Cardinal Melchior Tempi, the Apostolic Nuncio, a safe conduct letter, by the power of which Father Wyszyński was placed in a Reformati monastery of St. Peter of Alkantara in Lisbon, thus freeing him from Father Salazar.

Father Casimir could finally begin to put into effect the plans which had brought him to Portugal in the first place. Soon after he had arrived at the Reformati monastery, John of God of the Immaculate Conception was vested with the white Marian habit on March 25, 1754. This first Portuguese Marian was instrumental in establishing the Marian monastery in Balsamao.

Knowing about the existence of St. Francis tertiaries at the local sanctuary of the Blessed Mother, Fr. Casimir decided that they might join the Marians. He wrote a letter about the matter to the Bishop of Miranda, John of the Cross, a Carmelite, including information about the Marians and a picture of their Founder.

In his reply of July 1, 1754, the Bishop wrote to Father Casimir: *I received the letter and memorial of Your Reverence regarding the project of founding this new order in Balsamao. I did not respond immediately because I had to consider the entire project and obtain information about your institute, ask the opinion of the inhabitants of Balsamao and the pastor of the parish of Chacim. I enclose the letter of the superior of the house in Balsamao and the request of the hermits. For my part, I will not fail to assist you in any way, insofar as I am able, so that the project of Your Reverence may be realized. I think it is advisable that Your Reverence should go and take up residence there to allow the inhabitants to get to know you. I am certain that they will receive your Reverence with love because they wish to join an institute that has already been approved.*

The superior of the hermits in Balsamao was Father Hieronimus of the Holy Trinity, a very zealous and saintly priest. He not only attended to the tenor of the spiritual life of the tertiaries, but also to their finances and the outward appearance of the hermitage. Due to his efforts, the Stations of the Lord's Passion were built, which even today adorn the mountain and attract pilgrims from the area. Father Wyszyński vested him with the Marian habit. Then, accompanied by him and brother John of God, he made his way to Braganca, to the Bishop of Miranda, who was visiting there at the time. During their stay in Braganca, Father Hieronimus died having made his profession before Father Wyszyński, whom the Bishop now made the Superior of the hermitage in Balsamao.

In accord with a decree issued by the Ordinary of the

diocese on September 1, 1754, Father Casimir began the religious formation of the hermits of Balsamao. After six months of preparation, on April 13, 1755, he vested five Portuguese, one of which was a cleric, in minor orders, in the white Marian habit. Other candidates applied, too. Father Wyszyński acquainted them with the Marian rule and customs, and with the person of the Founder. By his words and by the example of his own life, he lay foundations for the permanent establishment of the Marians on Portuguese soil.

He felt, however, that the end of his laborious life was approaching. It was his desire that the ties between the Marians in Portugal and the headquarters of the Order in Poland would not be severed at the moment of his death. Therefore, he wrote to the Superior General: *We have to take into serious consideration the fact that this congregation, which will undoubtedly grow here, should not become separated from us after my death, due to a lack of contact with Poland ...*

Indeed, Father Casimir's fears quickly came true. On October 21, 1755, he left this world mourned by a small group of the Portuguese Marians. According to the local custom, he was buried on the same day in sand without a coffin, in the presence of only a few participants at the funeral. His body was placed under the floor of the church in Balsamao. It was only in 1759 that his earthly remains were exhumed from the sand and placed in a coffin in which they rested until 1955, when they were moved to a specially prepared

Foundation in Portugal 55

place in the wall of the church where they remain to this day.

Father Wyszyński's death was a great blow to the Portuguese Marians. They were left not only without a superior but also without a priest. None of them had made a profession by that time. They immediately besought the Superior General in Poland to have some Marians sent to continue the work begun by Father Casimir. It was only on March 8, 1758, that Father Alexy Fischer, a Czech, and Father Raphael de Buffa, an Italian, arrived at Balsamao. The Superior General, Father Cyprian Fijałkowski, had given Father Fischer full authority over the Marians in Portugal until his death on December 31, 1783. For some time later, the Portuguese Marians would contact the Polish Marians directly. Later, they did so through the Procurator General in Rome or through the Apostolic Nunciature in Lisbon. After 1798, when the Marians were expelled from Rome by the Napoleonic troops, such contacts came to an end altogether.

In the Vatican Archives, there are requests of the Portuguese Marians from the years 1819 to 1820 to be recognized as a separate branch of the Order with their own Superior General. Officially, however, they were left under the authority of the Superior General in Poland, even though the superiors in Balsamao were still referred to as "Superior Generals in the Kingdom of Portugal." The liquidation of religious orders in Portugal in 1843 put an end to their existence. The last "Superior General," Father Joseph of the Cross, left Balsamao in January of 1851 and died in his native village of Lagoa, not far from Balsamao, probably in 1856. It was only in 1955 that the Polish Marians arrived in Portugal to continue the work of Father Casimir Wyszyński. Presently, in 1985, there are 16 Marians, most of them of Portuguese descent, in three religious houses.

6. DEFENDER OF THE PEASANTS

The 18th century was a period in the history of Poland that saw the decline of the status of the peasants, the most numerous social class. Deprived of legal protection, they suffered most as a result of wars and frequent epidemics. Additionally, land was often taken away from the peasants and obligatory workloads on the lord's property increased. There were cases of peasants being sold in exchange for money or draft animals. Men of intellect called for reforms in this respect. Among others, Stanislaus Garczyński, the governor of the district of Poznań, wrote in the years 1733 to 1736 the famous *Anatomy of the Polish Republic*. In this book he exhorted the clergy to social works, in keeping with the Christian spirit, and to attend especially to the educational and cultural needs in the villages of the peasants.

This task was fulfilled to a certain degree by the Marians, who, for the most part, established their monasteries in the country, and who, in keeping with their goals, took care of the people who lived nearby. In the Marian Constitutions approved in 1723, there are instructions regarding the conducting of pastoral work through teachings and missions. It was emphasized there that many people in the Christian countries did not know the principles of faith, and because of the shortage of priests, the Marians, with the permission of the bishops, should teach the simple people the truths of the faith, both in their own churches and in the parish churches of the villages and towns. The instructions emphasize that such teaching should not involve debating complicated questions, but giving information necessary for salvation, namely: *so that they would get to know God, learn to love and praise Him, and to fulfill their Christian duties. These truths should be taught with such simplicity that all could understand. Therefore, beginning at the period of the novitiate, Marians should prepare themselves to teach Catechism and to preach useful sermons.*

On July 1, 1749, at the annual meeting presided over by Father Wyszyński, the superiors were obliged to ensure that Catechism was taught at their monasteries. This task was to be fulfilled by the clerics, and if there were none, by the promoters of the local fraternities or by the young priests. The catechesis would last four months, from the time when the period of Easter confessions was over till October. The classes were to be held every Sunday in the afternoon.

Father Wyszyński fulfilled these goals of the Marian vocation with a great zeal. In the beatification process of the Servant of God, the witnesses testified unanimously that he worked alongside the laborers at the construction of the monastery in Góra Kalwaria. He used this opportunity to teach them Catechism, singing with them to make their work less tedious. Father Taudt emphasized in his testimony that Father Wyszyński took care of the simple people: *Proclaiming God's Word to them, encouraging them to receive the holy sacraments, he assisted especially the poor and the abandoned.*

In Father Wyszyński's times, the Polish clergy, especially in the villages, did not always fulfill their tasks. There were cases where on the occasion of the Easter confession, the peasants were forced to work on the parish priest's property before they were admitted to the sacraments. These were times when there was a shortage of laborers due to wars or ravaging epidemics. Father Wyszyński wrote in his "Diary" on January 21, 1753, that he was *often heartbroken* to see that the peasants were so oppressed, even by the clergy. In addition to this, those busy at work on the priest's property and talking to each other could not prepare properly to the receive the sacraments, especially due to the fact that most of them did not know the basic truths of the faith. So they would return home from church *some all smiles, some gossiping, some quarreling.* Some would even get drunk at the inns *to the scandal of the non-believers and heretics.*

Father Wyszyński admits that he thought a lot about this matter when he was in Poland but could not find any way to make the lot of the peasants any easier. When he found himself in Rome, he visited the Holy Father and gave him a petition on behalf of the peasants. Then he would ask the religious coming from Poland whether there had been any changes for the better. Having found out that things were as they used to be, he decided to present a new memorial to the Pope. He remarked that he was not guided by any personal motives but by the desire to fulfill God's commandment which demands the love of neighbor and the care for his salvation. He suggested that the Pope might want to issue a special letter regarding this matter, either to the Apostolic Nuncio or to the Polish bishops in all dioceses. The Pope directed the drawing up of this petition to the Cardinal Secretary of State, and obligated him to gather the necessary information through the Nuncio in Poland. Father Wyszyński gave the memorial to Cardinal Valenti.

This memorial is now in the Vatican Archives. A copy of it was sent to the Apostolic Nuncio in Dresden, who, on February 19, 1753, wrote a letter to the Secretary of State, Cardinal Valenti: *There are many and serious disorders in the Kingdom of Poland, but it has never come to my attention what the memorial sent by Your Eminence concerns, namely that many parish priests do not admit the faithful to Easter confession and Holy Communion until they have worked for some time in their house, garden, or on their property. It is indeed a serious disorder but at the same time quite an unbelievable one. Nevertheless I shall try to obtain information which I will pass to Your Eminence in due time.*

After the matter had been investigated, it turned out that indeed there were abuses in some dioceses, particularly in places far away from the Bishop's seat. The Nuncio passed this message to the Vatican. At the same time, with Easter approaching, he decided to turn to the bishops on behalf of the Holy Father and call for putting an end to such abuses. The idea of sending a letter to all the bishops in Poland was considered, but given up as it might have painfully offended those bishops in whose dioceses there were no such abuses.

On May 8, 1753 the Nuncio wrote to the Secretary of State giving him more detailed information. The abuses mentioned earlier were practiced primarily in the dioceses of Gniezno, Cracow, Kujawy, Poznań, Płock, and Łuck. In answer to the intervention of the Apostolic Nuncio, special edicts were printed and published in particular dioceses. The copies of these edicts were sent to Rome.

On May 5, 1753, Pope Benedict XIV turned to the Apostolic Nuncio and encouraged him to write special letters to the bishops in whose dioceses the abuses regarding confessions were discovered. The Holy Father was going to send a letter to all the Polish bishops about the matter. When the letter from the Nuncio was read to the Pope in Castel Gandolfo on May 28th, he renewed his intention of sending a personal letter to the Polish bishops. It is not known whether such a letter was ever sent, because it has not been found in the Vatican Archives.

As Father Wyszyński emphasized in his "Diary", his heart bled when he saw the misery of the peasants. Attempting to lighten their burden even to some degree, he interceded on their behalf before the Pope. Sensitive to the injustice done to the peasants, he looked for justice at the highest level of moral authority in the Church. We are not certain whether Father Wyszyński ever learned about the positive results of his intercession before the Pope, since he was in Portugal at the time, making every effort to establish the Congregation of Marians in that country.

Father Wyszyński's social and pastoral activity is only one manifestation of his care for the peasants. To this should be added his personal influence on the magnates and representatives of the nobility with whom he made contacts and among whom the Marians worked. Introducing these people to the ways of Christian life must have undoubtedly left a mark on their attitudes towards the peasants.

Through his literary activity – although modest due to his active lifestyle – Father Casimir tried to reach the educated classes of the society and strengthen in them the appropriate principles of piety which, in turn, would shape their proper attitude towards life. One of the means leading to this end is a true devotion to the Blessed Virgin Mary. Father Wyszyński taught this to his fellow countrymen, drawing from the spiritual heritage of the Marians.

7. THE PROPAGATOR OF DEVOTION TO MARY

Father Casimir was a man of action and he would pick up a pen primarily for practical reasons. His "Records of the Activities in Rome and Notes Regarding the Canonization of the Founder," and his "Diary" are proof of the care he took to preserve and propagate the spiritual heritage of the Marians, and of his concern for their spiritual growth.

As already mentioned, Father Wyszyński was an ardent propagator of the devotion to Father Stanislaus Papczyński. During his stay in Rome and in Portugal, he wrote his biography which was supposed to introduce the person of the Founder of the Marians to other nations.

He translated the "Rule of the Marian Brothers of the Congregation of the Immaculate Conception of the Blessed Virgin Mary" from Latin into Polish. He attached to it questions and answers regarding religious vows, some remarks about the "Rule of the Ten Virtues of the Blessed Virgin Mary," and a short account about the Order of Marians. All of this was printed and published in 1750 in Warsaw.

Father Wyszyński is supposed to have written a book titled *Information About the Religious Article or the Scapular of the Immaculate Conception of the Blessed Virgin Mary Which is Given to People of All Social Standing by the Most Reverend Marian Fathers*. The book contains an account about the Marians, various prayers to the Blessed Mother Conceived without Sin, and prayers for the souls suffering in Purgatory. The book was published in 1773 in Berdyczów with a remark that it was already in its fourth edition. It is supposed that the first edition appeared in 1750.

The Propagator of Devotion to Mary 63

The purpose of Father Wyszyński's literary activity was not only to promote the order of the Marians but also to instill proper Christian attitudes in our country. We have already mentioned the book which he published in Rome about St. Ignatius of Antioch, a steadfast believer and martyr from the beginning of the second century of Christianity. Father Casimir's notes about the mystery of the Immaculate Conception, the priesthood, the religious life, the Word of God, and other truths of the faith, which are now in the Archives of the Sacred Congregation of Rites, were probably materials for an ascetic book.

Father Wyszyński came to love in a particular way the Immaculate Virgin Mary. When he joined the Order of Marians, he made efforts to bring about the growth of this Order for the greater glory of the Mother of God. He encouraged others to imitate Her virtues. To this end, he propagated information about the Marians and their rule of life. To this end, too, he published a book titled "Morning Star Rising Anew on the Polish Horizon" in 1749 in Warsaw.

Father Wyszyński mentions the fact that he had done a translation from Latin of a book by Francis Arias "De imitatione Mariae Virginis." But when the original text, which he edited in Rome in the years 1731 to 1733, is compared to the text in translation, it is possible to perceive considerable differences. He was not, then, a mere translator of someone else's thoughts, but poured on paper what he had meditated on himself, what he experienced and wanted to share with his readers. He adapted the book "Morning Star" not only to the Marian rule but also, as he himself points out on the title page, *to various groups of people, both religious and secular*. The 46-page long introduction which he wrote is an invaluable contribution enabling one to become acquainted with the Polish understanding of Mary in the 18th century. The enthusiasm of a zealous apostle and the propagator of a properly understood devotion to Mary Immaculate emanates from this introduction.

The truth about the Immaculate Conception of the Blessed Virgin Mary had not yet been proclaimed as a dogma of the faith, although it was the subject of reflection for theologians and the object of veneration for many Christians; even so, many religious orders, among them the Order of Marians, were founded to defend and propagate it. During his stay in Rome from 1751 to 1753, Father Wyszyński attentively followed everything concerning the devotion to the Immaculate Conception. He suffered because of the spread of Jansenism which attacked the Immaculate Conception of the Blessed Virgin Mary.

In his "Diary" dated September 7, 1751, Father Wyszyński made a remark about a book which questioned the Immaculate Conception of the Blessed Virgin Mary as a contemptible superstition. The book created many doubts so that *even some of our Order gave in to this ridicule*. Although Father Joannes a Luca Venetus thoroughly refuted these accusations, the contrary opinion *among the wise of this world still lingers.* It pained him that, due to the lack of funds, Abbot Louis Andruzzi could not publish his work titled "Perpetua Ecclesiae doctrina de Immaculata Conceptione Beatae Virginis Mariae" (The Church's Eternal Teaching on the Immaculate Conception of the Blessed Virgin Mary).

It was a great joy for Father Wyszyński to meet Pope Benedict XIV, which he mentions in his "Diary" dated November 29, 1751: *It was only today ... that I was fortunate to be received by the Pope. As it was my desire to attain this honor, I put pusillanimity aside. Moved by zeal and being the Procurator of the order, I asked for my name to be entered in the register as Padre Procuratore Generale di Religiosi Mariani ... Polacco. Requesting an audience as such, I was received, I gave the Holy Father a report on our order, on my duties and activities, and I asked his blessing for our congregation. The Holy Father answered: "Benedico tibi et Congregationi" (I bless you and the Congregation). Then I said: This Congregation was founded for the greater honor of the Immaculate Virgin. The Holy Father asked: "Immaculate Conception? Good!" And he nodded.*

Father Wyszyński's insistence that the Marians not miss an opportunity for the beatification of their Founder took into account the possibility of expediting the solemn promulgation of the dogma of the Immaculate Conception. On February 26, 1752, he wrote in his "Diary": *They are urging us to begin efforts for the elevation of our Founder to the honors of the altar. That would help us to refute the attacks of the enemies of this holy mystery, and the Holy Church would have a reason to proceed with the definitive pronouncement of this truth. I am here like a thorn in the side of these enemies, so they do not like to look at me, but we expect to conquer all these adversities soon, as long as we all become worthy of and favorable to the promotion of the honor of the Most Holy Virgin.*

In his letter addressed to the Superior General, Father Kajetan Wetycki, dated July 15, 1752, Father Wyszyński returns to this matter: *Nobody hides the candle under a bushel basket, but puts it on a stand, so it can give light. If we want the order of the Virgin Mary to flourish, we should busy ourselves with noble and praiseworthy deeds. We are not the concern here, rather, the honor of the Immaculate Conception of the Blessed Virgin Mary is. Therefore, her order should be spread, and the venerator of this mystery, our venerable father, should be particularly praised, and efforts should be made to bring about his beatification. He deserved it and is worthy of it, and it is our duty to do this for him. Nobody will condemn us, rather they will praise us for it. The Lord God Himself demands this from us when He blesses us unexpectedly in many things whenever we do what we intended in the beatification cause of our Founder.*

In his aforementioned introduction to "Morning Star," Father Wyszyński emphasizes that devotion to Mary is one of many graces which God bestowed upon the Polish nation. The manifestations of this devotion are the churches, altars, pictures, religious orders, and fraternities dedicated to the Mother of God. The devout *give constant praise to her honor in prayers, hymns, and songs, and ask her intercession with God in their needs, relying on her most effective help ... There are many faithful, too, who undertake the effort to make pilgrimages to her holy and miraculous pictures. There is also quite a number of women and men who, having abandoned the goods of this world, give themselves to Mary for the eternal service in the religious orders under her name ... Many a time did the Polish knights enter a fight with the enemies of her holy name ...*

The imitation of Mary's virtues and life must be added as the most important feature to all these manifestations of the devotion to her. She was endowed by God in a particular way. Jesus praised His mother for listening to the word of God ardently and keeping it in the practice of everyday life. Hence, Father Casimir emphasizes what St. Augustine had declared, namely, that Mary was much more blessed due to her deep faith than due to the fact that she was the mother of God.

The Servant of God reminds his countrymen: *...if we want to show real veneration for the Virgin Mary and be her servants, it is not enough to have knowledge about her majesty, nobility, privileges, and virtues with which she shined. We must not be satisfied with simply proclaiming her praise in prayers and hymns, with making sacrifices* *and vows, but we must imitate her life and virtues whereby we will become like her and thus liked by her. I write after St. John: "He who says he abides in Christ, ought to walk in the same way in which He walked." (1 John 2, 6). Similarly, he who would associate himself with Mary, ought to imitate her virtues and walk the way she walked, following Christ. This is how true venerators of Mary, whom she acknowledges, may be recognized, and it is expressed in the Book of Sirach in these words: "Whoever obeys me, will not be put to shame, and those who work with my help will not sin." (Sirach 24, 22). Hence it is evident that we venerate Mary most perfectly when we imitate her virtues as described in the Gospels.*

Father Wyszyński emphasizes later: *We want to point only to ten of the evangelical virtues of the Virgin Mary to be imitated. Although our Most Beloved Lady shined with countless virtues, apart from these ten, they would be not only difficult to imitate but also difficult to understand, for she surpassed in virtues not only the most holy of people, but even angels.* By using various comparisons, Father Casimir wanted to show the precise meaning of the Virgin Mary's virtues for the Christian life. He remarks that they are a kind of talent given by God, which can be redoubled by imitating them. They are lamps with which the whole world can be illuminated. They are capable of purifying not only the ten lepers, but also all sinners. For we are all in need of God's mercy: *By imitating the Mother of God we will obtain forgiveness for our sins, God's mercy, and deliverance from the hands of the enemies of our soul and of our earthly life, who all lie in wait, especially in recent times, for the undoing of our distressed Homeland.*

Mary is the "Morning Star" which leads to Christ, the "Sun of Justice." Father Wyszyński got the idea of such a title for the book written by Arias from St. Bernard. he quotes his words: *She is the noble Star rising from the House of Jacob, whose rays illuminate the whole world, and this light shines high above, penetrating the depths and piercing the earth. It warms the soul more than the body, it preserves virtues and destroys bad habits. She is the brightest and the most magnificent Star above the vast sea of the world, shining with virtues and illuminating with merits. If someone is immersed in the turbulent waters of this world more than he walks on the earth, he should not turn his eyes away from this Star if he does not want to drown. When the gales of temptations rise against you and you fall into the trap of your senses, look up to this Star, call upon Mary. When anger, greed, or covetousness shake the boat of your mind, look to Mary. When you become inundated by the waves of pride, insolence, slander and hatred, look at the Star, call upon Mary. When you become distressed by the number of your sins, ashamed of the impurity of your conscience, frightened by the harshness of the judgment, and plunged in the abyss of sadness, think on Mary. When you are oppressed, or in danger, or besieged by doubts, remember her and call upon her name. May it never disappear from your lips or withdraw from your heart. Follow her example if you want to receive her help. If you imitate her, you shall never lose your way. You will not be disappointed if you ask her. If you think about her, you will not commit a sin. You will not fall when she supports you. Under her care, you will not be afraid. You will not get tired when she leads you. You will reach your destination with her help and guidance. (Hom. 2 super Missus est, sub finem).*

This quotation demonstrates Father Wyszyński's familiarity with the opinions of popular writers about the Blessed Mother. From himself Father Wyszyński added: *Let us, then, watch the rise and the movements of this brightest Star carefully; Let us follow her; Let us rise up from the sleep of death by sin. If we want to see this Morning Star rising, we must zealously imitate the Ten Virtues of the Virgin Mary. For just as a star once led the three wise men to Jesus as He lay in a stable in Bethlehem, so will this Morning Star, shining with the ten rays of these evangelical virtues, lead us to Jesus sitting at the right hand of the Father in the heavenly kingdom. For Mary is the living Star of the evangelical law and of the Holy Church, and her example should be followed by all the faithful. Those, who by Satan's deceit were persuaded to break God' ten commandments, will resist the evil spirit by imitating these ten virtues and will thus be spiritually reborn.*

As it has been mentioned before, Father Wyszyński reworked Arias' masterpiece adapting it to the "Rule of the Ten Virtues of the Blessed Virgin Mary," by which the

Marians were bound at that time. Therefore, he combined the chapters of this book written by the Spanish Jesuit into ten separate "treatises," each being dedicated to a different virtue.

In this manner the following virtues are discussedć chastity, prudence, humility, faith, devotion, obedience, poverty, patience, charity, and the sorrows of the Most Holy Virgin Mary. Such an outline for this book, prepared for print by Father Wyszyński, seems to be a continuation of the thought of the Founder of the Marians.

Father Papczyński wrote a work "Templum Dei Mysticum" (The Mystical Temple of God) which contains the principles of life to be followed by any Christian who truly wants to be a temple of God. Virtues are the ornaments of this temple.

Father Wyszyński discussed in greater detail their participation in the spiritual development of man. He also emphasized that, because of these virtues, Mary has a share in the work of the redemption of the world. He wrote: *When we recall the virtues with which the Virgin Mary crushed the head of the dragon from Hell, we fill all of Hell with fear. By imitating and practicing these virtues, the faithful cannot stray from the path to salvation for they receive deliverance and help from their Lady.*

Evidently, even in Father Wyszyński's times there were many who opposed devotion to Mary, referring to the duty to imitate only Jesus Christ. Therefore, Father Casimir quoted the words of St. Paul encouraging us to embrace Christ's own attitude, adding: *Since the Doctor of the Nations tells us to imitate him and other Apostles because he and the others imitated Christ, why then shouldn't we imitate Mary who was closest to Christ and most intimately involved in the matters of His life ... Furthermore, we are to imitate Mary not only in the manner that she imitated Christ the Lord, but also in all things to which He, being both God and man, was not obliged. We are to respect and love Him, trust Him and believe in Him. In our gratitude for the grace of redemption, we should imitate not Christ, but Mary — the first participant of redemption, free from the stain of the Original Sin.*

Could it not be, then, that Father Wyszyński's thought about changing the world through a true and complete devotion to Mary be applied to our own times? *I gave the book on the imitation of the evangelical virtues of the Virgin Mary the title "Morning Star" because I saw how the entire world is plunged in evil, has many bad habits, is unaware of what is good and beneficial, and through its mistakes and heresies becomes separated from Christ — the Sun of Justice. Just like the morning star, Aurora, announces the rising of the Sun, so will the virtues of the Virgin Mary point the way to Christ, the Sun of Justice, for those who readily undertake to practice them.*

8. AWAITING THE BEATIFICATION

The conditions in which Father Casimir lived and worked were difficult. The period under Saxon rule was one of widespread material, spiritual, and moral degradation. The spiritual emptiness and mediocrity were covered up with the glamour and the lavish lifestyle of the upper classes of the society. To attain their misconceived ideal, the rich did not hesitate to oppress the least fortunate and impose ever heavier burdens upon the peasants. Father Wyszyński, witnessing the practices of the times did not give up the fight to change this situation, he never lost hope.

In this regard, he reminisced of St. Augustine, who said to those Christians frightened by the collapse of Rome in the year 410: *You are crying that the world is coming to an end, that bad times are coming! Have you already forgotten the words of the Savior: "Heaven and earth will pass away, but my words will never pass away." We are the times. The times are such as we are. The barbarians will not take away what is guarded by Christ. The Vandals cannot kill our true life.*

Father Casimir went about his own life with similar faith and courage. If the times are a reflection of the way we are, then we need to grow in goodness and steadfastly follow the chosen path. Therefore, Father Casimir carefully guarded the faith which he received in his family home. Guided by the spirit of faith, he undertook a pilgrimage to far away Rome which resulted in his becoming tied with a religious order founded not far from his own birthplace.

He soon learned that not everything was ideal in this order. But he did not leave it in search of a better one. He was able to overcome the obstacles, to wait, and to prepare himself patiently for new tasks and duties. He gave a splendid example to all of us, who so often give in to impatience, resignation, indifference, and flee from difficulties.

He began the work of improving the Order by beginning with himself, with a steadfast realization of the ideal of the Marian life. With his eyes on Mary, the "Morning Star", imitating her virtues according to the "Rule of the Ten Virtues" by which the Marians were bound, he became more and more united with Christ.

At present, we do not have access to the documents concerning Father Casimir's beatification process in which the witnesses testify to his heroic virtues. On the basis of his biography and of own his writings which are available to us, we can infer that everything he taught to others was a most precious treasure to himself as well. He educated generations of young Marians, pointing to Mary as a sign of victory of God's grace over human weakness. He called upon them to imitate Mary. He encouraged the faithful to deepen their devotion to Mary, he showed them the way to follow the "Morning Star."

The virtues which he discussed according to the order

of the "Rule of the Ten Virtues of the Blessed Virgin Mary" were very close to his heart. When reading the introduction to "Morning Star", one has the impression that all the advice contained there comes from Father Casimir's own experience. Here is a fragment of what he wrote in his introduction:

It is my advice to all those who truly and sincerely desire to practice the virtues necessary for salvation, that they first eradicate the bad habits and customs that are contrary to virtue, so that they might be able to grow in virtue. Furthermore, they must avoid temptations and opportunities for evil.

1. For we cannot consider someone to be chaste if he frivolously puts his chastity at risk; if he does not resist temptations bravely and calmly looks at what is indecent; if he does not discipline his body by fasting, by keeping vigils, and by moderation in food and drink.

2. How can one consider himself prudent who does not know how to restrain his tongue, so that he would not say anything against God, neighbor, or virtue; who does not avoid vain and false words; who does not control his laughter and who does not discipline himself to behave in a dignified manner with an attitude befitting a child of God?

3. How can one consider himself humble who puts himself above others and ignores his neighbor; who avoids menial tasks and, if obliged to perform them, does so with great sadness, dislike, and complaints?

4. How can one be deeply faithful who has doubts about the truth of the holy faith and who does not do what faith demands? For faith consists not so much in meditation and words but in fulfilling the orders of our holy religion.

5. How can one be considered pious who, out of laziness, does not attend services; who spends more time in idleness than in prayer and, when he prays, his thoughts wander goodness only knows where; who forgets that God is present everywhere; and who breaks God's commandments as well as those of the Church?

6. How can one be obedient who does not obey the orders of his parents, superiors, and teachers; and who acts only because he is under constraint to do so or because it is convenient to him; and who recoils from doing anything that is contrary to his likes and whims? The virtue of obedience consists in doing what we are ordered to do and not what we might prefer.

7. How can one be called poor in spirit whose heart clings to worldly possessions as if they comprised the very purpose of his life, setting all his hopes on them rather than on God; or who, bound by the vow of poverty, still seeks to have what he should forgo and, when he finds himself poor and in need, complains and does not accept God's Will for him?

8. How can one be considered patient who does not gladly accept the adversities and crosses which God sends him in His graciousness so that he might be perfected, but who instead complains or even curses Him? And who, having suffered something from his neighbor, takes revenge or desires to do so?

9. How can one be considered charitable or merciful who does not perform acts of mercy; who does not take pity on his neighbor or help him in his need, when the opportunity arises; who does not pray for his neighbors and who does not come to the rescue of the souls suffering in Purgatory by participating in Masses, by prayer and by giving alms?

10. And, finally, how can one feel compassion for Christ Crucified and take pity on Him in His Passion who does not recall the tremendous grace of redemption and everything that Christ suffered for him and ponder it with sincere gratitude; who does not deplore the fact that so many souls redeemed by His Precious Blood perish; and who is not the least bit concerned that the number of the enemies of the of Christ's Cross is growing, as if all of this did not cost Christ Our Lord anything and as if it did not hurt Him at all?

So how can they consider themselves venerators of the Virgin Mother of God who do not acquire the virtues with which Mary shines, but only talk about them?

These ardent recommendations flowed from the soul of a man who put into action what he proclaimed by his words. Portuguese authors describing the person of Father Wyszyński on the basis of the testimony of witnesses, stated that he lived a saintly life. They all emphasized his perfect love of God, which found expression in the particularly careful manner in which he prepared to celebrate the Holy Mass. People who lived far away from Balsamao hastened there to see the "Santo Polacco," the Saintly Pole, at the altar.

He lived a life full of mortification. Throughout his 30 years of religious life, he slept only five hours a day and he wore a hair shirt all the time. His attitude towards others expressed a special love of neighbor. He was kind, and he forgave every wrong and unpleasantness done to him with all his heart. He readily fulfilled his pastoral duties. He wanted to influence wide circles of Polish society by the spiritual rebirth of his own order, to which he himself greatly contributed.

The Primate of the Millennium* emphasized Father Casimir's role in awakening the hope for the nation's survival due to the particular protection of Mary: *To a nation of people who were losing their freedom, Father Casimir revealed their very Mother. He tied this nation personally to her through the veneration of her Immaculate Conception and Sorrowful Heart. He began to preach to the nation that all abandon themselves to Mary's maternal bondage...He trusted that everything entrusted to her care would never perish.*

Although Father Wyszyński did appreciate the importance of the outward manifestations of devotion to Mary,

---

*Translator's note: The Primate of the Millennium was Cardinal Stefan Wyszyński.

he pointed out that it was a change of Christian life that was necessary. Therefore, he attempted to incorporate in Marian devotions the practice of imitating Mary's attitude as it was expressed in her relation to God, her love of Christ, and in the manner she lived her life, according to the teachings of the Gospel. Such an emphasis was necessary as much in the 18th century as it is today. For one cannot forget Christ's warning that it is not enough to praise God with our lips and be satisfied merely with the outward manifestations of the faith. It is the effort to fulfill God's will in every sphere of our lives that gives us the guarantee of salvation. This is the attitude that Mary teaches us. Therefore, we should stake everything on Mary as she is the Morning Star that points to Christ, the Sun of Justice.

Imitating the attitude of Christ's Mother leads us to be more closely tied to the lives of others. Her eyes noticed the needs of others, they saw the humble and the hungry *whom God fills with good things*. Throughout his entire life, Father Wyszyński steadfastly strove after holiness, and Mary Immaculate, the Morning Star showed him the way. People saw his holiness, and were drawn to him to seek his support. Meeting him prompted them to work at their own improvement and to be kind to others. On the basis of his biography, it may be concluded that he contributed a lot to the rebirth of the nation; he tried to overcome the decline of the Saxon epoch. His influence reached beyond the borders of his homeland, which he loved and whose welfare he desired.

He spent merely a few months in Portugal, but it is there that the memory of him survives so strongly to this day. Soon after his death, the Portuguese took steps to begin the cause for his beatification. Despite the liquidation of the religious orders in Portugal, and despite the fact that the church and monastery in Balsamao were left unattended, pilgrims kept coming to the grave of the "Saintly Pole". Much was written about him in Portugal, yet he was little known in his own homeland.

As early as August 4, 1756, the Bishop of Miranda issued a decree announcing the commencement of the information process regarding Father Casimir's virtues and the miracles obtained through his intercession. Soon afterwards, the Bishop died, and it became necessary to wait until September 29, 1763 for any actual proceedings in this matter to begin. Eighty-five witnesses of Father Wyszyński's life were interviewed in Miranda. A similar process was conducted in Lisbon where eight witnesses gave their testimony, and in Poland where nine people testified to the heroism of Father Casimir's virtues.

In 1771, the files containing these testimonies were sent to Rome. In 1780, the Sacred Congregation of Rites issued a decree allowing the appointment of a committee to formally conduct the beatification process of Father Casimir in this Congregation. The beatification cause progressed rather swiftly. Many witnesses were convinced that they had received graces through the intercession of the Servant of God. The reknown of his holiness spread

Awaiting the Beatification

ever farther, and requests for his speedy elevation to the honors of the altar came, from King Augustus III, from the Patriarch of Jerusalem, from the Superior Generals of the Franciscans and the Piarists, and from many of the magnates from Poland.

The Napoleonic wars and the expulsion of the Marians from Rome interrupted any further developments in this matter. It was resumed only in 1953. From then through the year 1985, detailed investigations were carried out in the archives in Poland, Portugal, and Rome, on the basis of which Rev. Boleslaus Jakimowicz wrote a book (*Positio*), printed and published in Rome in November of 1985.

This book provided a sufficient basis for the Historical Section of the Congregation for Saints and its expert historians to become acquainted with the life and activity of Father Wyszyński. Then, in 1989, after more historical scrutiny by the Congregation for Saints, the Holy See recognized the heroic virtues of the Servant of God Father Casimir, who now bears the title of "Venerable." Thus, a miracle obtained by his intercession and recognized as such by the Holy See, is now the only thing necessary for his beatification.

What does "Venerable Servant of God" mean? It means that after thoroughly examining all the available evidence, the Church had found sufficient proof that the person in question has reached such a state of holiness that he or she acted consistently with perfect virtue.

The renown of the Venerable Servant of God Father Casimir's holiness, which survives to this day, gives us reason to hope for the successful conclusion of the efforts in his beatification cause. Therefore, we trustingly await a speedy elevation to the honors of the altar of a man who showed us how to conquer evil with good; how to model one's spiritual life after the example of the Blessed Mother through the imitation of her virtues; how to stake everything on Mary so that the Kingdom of her Son would grow.

9. PRAYER FOR THE BEATIFICATION

Most holy and undivided Trinity, You choose to live in the hearts of Your faithful servants, and after their death to reward their merits with the glory of heaven. Grant, we implore You, that Your Servant Casimir, who with apostolic zeal faithfully served the Church under the patronage of the Immaculate Virgin Mary, may be numbered among the Blessed, through Christ our Lord. Amen.

10. PRAYER FOR A SPECIAL GRACE

O God, Merciful Father, in the heart of Your Servant Casimir You aroused such a great zeal for accomplishing corporal and spiritual deeds of mercy; deign to grant me (to us) through his intercession the grace ... for which I (we) implore You ... Amen.
Our Father ... Hail Mary ... Glory be to the Father

Note : It is recommended that this prayer, recited for a particular intention, be complemented by Confession and Holy Communion.

Information about graces received through the intercession of the Venerable Servant of God, Father Casimir Wyszyński, and applications from those wishing to become priests or brothers – followers of Mary Immaculate in the service of Christ and the Church, in the Congregation of the Marians – should be sent to the following address:

Br. Andrew R. Mączyński, MIC
Vice-Postulator of the
Marian Causes of Canonization
Eden Hill
Stockbridge, MA 01263

An 18th Century portrait of Fr. Casimir from Portugal, painted by A. Padrão. The Venerable Servant of God's heroic perseverance led to the founding of a Marian community in Balsamão, Portugal, and the international expansion of the Order.

Another 18th Century portrait of the Venerable Servant of God which is on display at the monastery in Balsamão, Portugal.

Hair shirt or cilice used for mortification by Fr. Casimir. Such a device was commonly used by clergy and religious of the day to mortify the flesh. A certificate of authenticity is displayed with the hair shirt.

Detail of Fr. Casimir in a group portrait of White Marians with the Virgin Mary depicted as the Immaculate Conception. The 18th Century painting is displayed at the Marian monastery in Balsamão, Portugal.

Fr. Casimir's personal cutlery. These are some of his personal effects which are on display at the Marian monastery in Balsamão, Portugal. A certificate attests to their authenticity.

The beads on which Fr. Casimir recited the Chaplet of the Ten Virtues of the Most Blessed Virgin Mary. He found meditation and prayer upon the Ten Virtues of the Blessed Virgin Mary to be a great source of spiritual strength and consolation.

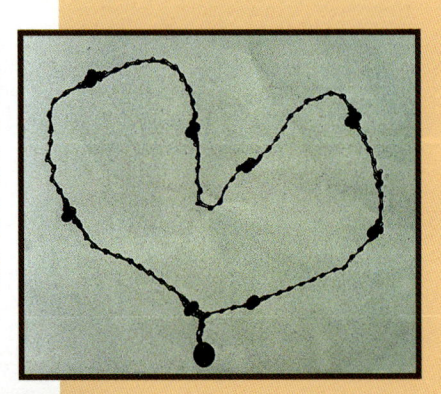

The baptismal font in Fr. Casimir's native parish in Jeziórka near Grójec. In all likelihood, this is where the Venerable Servant of God was baptized.

This engraving in brass is a tribute to the life and work of Fr. Casimir. The engraving is anonymous and the work of art is from the 18th century.

The frame of Fr. Casimir's bed in his simple cell at the monastery in Balsamão, Portugal. Fr. Casimir was known for his austere, monastic lifestyle.

This portrait of Fr. Casimir and Our Lady shows Mary holding the Scapular of the Immaculate Conception of the Blessed Virgin Mary, commonly called the Blue Scapular. The Venerable Servant of God zealously promoted this devotion to Mary Immaculate.

The coffin of Fr. Casimir which used to contain his earthly remains. It is on display in the Marians' monastery church at Balsamão, Portugal. Many of the faithful visit this church and invoke the intercession of the Venerable Servant of God for personal favors and graces from God.